THE CENTRAL EYE

THE CENTRAL EYE

JUDITH YARNALL

Other Books by Judith Yarnall

Transformations of Circe
Poems of Karacaoglan, trans. with Seyfi Karabas

Onion River Press
89 Church Street
Burlington, VT 05401

info@onionriverpress.com
www.onionriverpress.com

ISBN: 978-1-966607-01-4
Library of Congress Control Number: 2025909242

In grateful memory

Dorothy Francis Hollenbach
Victor Swenson
Katherine True

Contents

Foreword

I'm a persistent rather than prolific poet. The poems included here were written over several decades of my adult life. Generally, the poems in the first section, Childhoods, date back the furthest and the poems in Grief Sequence are the most recent. Several generations of family, seen from widening perspectives, are part of this collection. I'm the link with the pen.

In choosing and arranging poems for publication, I realized that my obsessions have been more constant than style and voice. I chose not to bring the poem's references to technology and fashion up to date. Slides projected on a kitchen wall? Preppy clothes in high school halls? These details and others remain true to their origins. Poetry itself has been the true constant, a challenge and a leavening. I'm inspired by the words of the French poet Paul Éluard, "there is another world, but it is in this one."

CHILDHOODS

Daybreak I

Your howl like an abandoned cat's
penetrates my sleep.
Mumbling, I rush to your side
find you already gone bleary with rage,
thin newborn's limbs
bent tight as fists.

Gathering you to my streaming breasts
I trail quilts to the rocker, where we
conspire against darkness and cold,
the raw March of this ancient house.
In the barn across the road
someone's dawn snaps on.

Gradually you loosen
and calm, settle into your hunger.
Small expert, second child
how surely you get what you want.
        I yawn and drift out
towards the stars, mild in their great black sea,
uncaught in identity
until your rooting pulls me back.

And now you pause to look up at me,
milk running down your chin, and
pleasure quietly, wholly as light
glides across your face.

Children's Questions

1.

What grade are you in when you die?

Not remembering the small victims
of plagues and bombs, I told Jake Grade 13
and it lasts the rest of your life.

I meant to reassure him,
offer a sweet of half-truth,
but he had his own ways of search.

That afternoon he hid in the cellar
and would not answer to his name.

Hours later, I gathered him
into my shaking arms.

2.

Where did Victor go?

two-year old Oliver asked his mom
when she told him
she was writing me an email.

I thought of all the times
grandchildren had appeared at our door,
stepping into my welcoming arms
even as they asked *where's Victor?*

as if they had some special radar,
some sonic magic that picked up beams
from a kindred being in a distant room.
No matter that he now had trembling hands
and arthritic knees, no longer sprawled
by train sets or crawled after
squealing toddlers.

Beep, I think they heard,
I'm here like you,
born into this wondrous playground.

3.
What if we had no weather?

For Steven, whose musing
stunned a dinner table—well,
who was ready to launch into this void
of no buds, no warmth, no snow
no howling winds to shake the trees
and blow boredom from our souls?

Not we grownups, who sat there imagining
a colorless, northern, paused April
while our children romped through ether.

An ether that extended,
as I learned later from my youngest daughter,
into the cloudy and glorious regions of pre-birth.
At supper her sisters were chatting
about something that happened before
she joined us, an Easter egg hunt perhaps
when they were three and six,
too low to the ground to spy
the rose and violet treasures nestled
in crotches of trees, waiting
to be found in August.

       No, Anna exploded,
I remember. I was always here.
How do you know I wasn't?

Whose Shoes

They're still as soft as the infant who
wore them, nearly a century later,
five pearl buttons down each side
ankle-high leather of creamy mocha
and a tiny acorn stamped on each sole—
their mysterious owner soon too big
to give them a decent scuffing.

Was it my father in 1914,
who grew up to be a basketball star
suffering his own Great Depression
before he steadied to a job at the mill
and the nurture of chosen joys?

Or my grandmother in 1879,
apprenticed years later to a dressmaker
when her family lost its land?
Whom I twirled before as a hemless child
while her mouth bristled with pins.

These shoes, this child, soft as my own,
besting us all by lasting.

My Fossil Kate

Small caterwauler caught
In infancy's cocoon,
All wrapped in rage. You fought
With clawing hands and siren lungs,
Spewing sour milk, you sought
Uncurdled love.

You clung. I was your tree.
Prehensile weight slung curve to curve,
You rebecame a part of me.
Through a hundred kitchen six o'clocks,
Never content to solely be,
You hung, my fifth most cumbrous limb.

Who would have thought your mind, in thrall
To need, could ever freely play?
That you, fierce rejecter of all
Not succor and bole, would seek
The world's rough edges, fall
Prey to curiosity?

And, with interest undomiciled,
Rove eyes over smooth zebra rocks
Of slate and quartz which so beguiled

The rest of us, to settle them
On stony mud? Excavating child,
Finder of Silurian shellprints,

Explorer of the Champlain Sea,
You are trapped in memory's
Bedrock as you once were in self—
Fossil raging babe to me.

Fever

We sit in the late winter light,
you ripened by fever to a beauty
of blooming cheeks and blazing eyes,
propped on pillows beside me.
Like conspirators entering a dark wood
we leaf through *The Juniper Tree*.
I read recipes for grim metamorphoses:
how to make logs from insolent girls
and stews of curious boys,
how to compost with bone and ash
the fat white root of happiness,
that it might split and flower.

At tales' end
I smooth damp hair
away from your temples,
then pick up crumbs of the ordinary
and follow them to the kitchen
where I stir our supper soup.
You, fed by your fire, turn round
in your forest for sleep.

On Julia's Clothes

No one wears silks in high school halls.
Instead, you opt for well-cut denim
oxford cloth and Shetland wool,
the undeniable satisfaction
of numinous labels on quiet clothes.

Do your perfect breasts and tawny limbs
shine through this camouflage?
or do you walk those corridors
unnoticed, because you look just right?

Song for Julia

Walk fearlessly, well loved one
Plant your tanned feet
in the sands of Assateague
as you did when you were one.
Be again that child who never looked back
as she walked the fluid boundary
where the oceans of the world roll in,
and then swerved into the breakers.

Walk mindfully, well loved one
Be confident in your rescues.
Feed deeply on trust.
Gather what is small and imperiled
into the home of your arms.

The Enchantress

for Annalivia

Who could resist such wild, wild eyes
articulate eyebrows, sour smiles—
certainly not your mother.
And so, my gap-toothed faerie queen,
I pray that you may find
friends and lovers of equal power,
not just pale loiterers;
that never may you trap yourself
within your hills and rings,
that all your spells be gay and grave
that mercy will become you.

Morning Child

1.

Warm in her rumpled bednest
rosy, sensient, caressed
by her parents' providence,
she lies calm, beyond offense,
her smile infinite as the sea
uncaught in identity.

2.

A two-years' hoard of self beleaguered
by outsized marauders eager
to force her beg cereal with "please"
just to appease their grownup whims,
in fury she hurls brickbats of will
against the four-walled world.

Fourteen, August

Maples trembling with breeze
and sunlight. Inside, the babble of soaps.
An angular girl sunk deep in a couch,
enthralled by blue-scrubbed adulterers.

At break a gingerly tearing
of roots, a slow scan of the fridge
as she grips her left instep and coolly extends—
a palm, a Siberian iris.

There's nothing to eat.
The door swings shut. She walks past
vistas of shimmering trees,
back to the days of her life.

Eleven

for Anabel Dwyer

In that spring long ago
we taught each other flight.
I boosted you up in a hickory,
charmed the creek waters almost still
and said the words which would make you
leap, shinnying into air.
As you swooped
and rose again and again
I felt the rope burn my hands
and I knew the moment
you chose to fall,
laughing, to the shadowed pool.

Now I see only dandelions—
golden, idealized fields
with dresses spread out to dry.
Two children lying on budding chests
among the sashes and flowers.

But even then we were ravenous,
passing out secrets like grapes:
what boy told you
he liked me, who was going with who,
what girl got out of gym
on grounds of mysterious illness.

Already I think we longed
to cross over, to let
love take on substance and gender,
        to bleed and kiss and wear
round our necks
class rings like bright lumps of coal.

We rose, put
on our lives,
went back home for supper.
You were grey-eyed, near as sunlight.
How easily we let go.

Fifth Grade

In Miss Hollweg's class
no one was bored
We left our suburban gridiron streets
for the jungles of Yucatan

Page after page we followed her voice
on the trail of Halliburton
to Aztec altars and deep stone pools,
a virgin's still-beating heart

Beneath bronze curls and bows at her neck
something manic lay coiled
She hurled a book at Ricky Fidler
What would happen next?

It was a year of horizons and water balloons
of a strange, dawning pity
We left our suburban gridiron streets
for the jungles of Yucatan

The Guardian

You, grandfather, baptized me,
opened the terrible ground,
taught me what I couldn't bear
that winter when I was three.
         One morning, early,
you rose and were felled,
struck clean through the heart.
Called home to God, they told me later
to live with the saints and angels.
I understood only enough
to recognize the lie.

For your life was mine,
we had sealed our vows with
a hundred nuptial cigar rings,
whirled round the world across our floor,
collapsed on the beach of a sofa.
I laughed myself calm within your arms,
free and protected at last.

Your brought me the sun
congealed in jars, from a store
on your route from the mill.
Its combs floated, suspended in gold,
waiting to burst on my tongue.
         Because of you I trusted
feasts, and the gentleness of men.

And then you turned to nothing
and my child's heart froze.

Now, a long winter past,
I think again about death.
How and from where have I called
you up, from what bower of darkness?
For you've stood for months
by this lonely bed - a modest and faithful shade
drawn by our bond of blood.

      Stay, be my muse
for love, for the brink.
Lend the abyss a face.

Reticence and Words

1. It is probably 1920.
I make you out
from the photograph's grain,
a still and dark-eyed child
on the steps of a country school.
Like the others you wear
gingham and lisle, long white stockings
wrinkling at the knees,
a preposterous bow pinned to your bob.
Nothing suggests
your orphan's knowledge.

You stare seriously
back at the lens and beyond
to the valley in spring,
the dirt lanes and creek
you will follow home,
the animals pastured in
April light.

Cherry and pale boughs
of dogwood
wreathe the broken fields.

2. Long before my memory
has formed, my mother
walks in her rose garden.
She is eighteen or
twenty or twenty-five,
serene as Aphrodite
when the sea first fell
from her limbs.

Her hair is loose,
beaded with rain,
the shears are bright in her hand
as she moves from bush to bush,
fingering the barbed stems.

Mutely the flowers
incline towards her
their faces of bruisable silk,
their furled reserves of scarlet,
the power of their names.

Ophelia, Peace
the Queen of Snow,
eglantine for its wildness—
in a trance she gathers
and clips them all.
Roses spill from her arms.

Later they bloom in light-filled rooms,
their passion arranged to
a scented calm.
                    Even now
our lives are tinged.

3. When my brother brought in
the day-old birds
it was she who took them
for her own, warming them
in the nest of her palms,
cradling their downless sticky flesh
till the yolk-sacs beat
with survival.

Soon enough
the pasted eyes opened
to beady glares, and
maws poured forth incessantly
their foul music of hunger.
It must have pared
at my mother's bones

But she went on poking
milk-soaked crumbs
down each frail throat in turn,
smoothing scruffy pinfeathers
as she looked ahead
to flight.

4. I watched her come up
the cellar stairs
great with a basket of laundry

it was her third ascension
of the day and she was
whistling   always whistling

as she pinned cotton underwear
next to socks
next to bedsheets and lace-trimmed slips

as she went inside
and waited for the wind
with its sweet and diligent breath

and returned to the yard
and took it all down
made compact balls of the mates

while her mouth
drawn tight like a marblebag
let out its stuttered songs

5. As I drifted towards sleep
you would rise from my side,
each time crossing to the darkened window
to let in the cool night air.

Always, the trees lay in wait:
sycamores with moon-silvered bones,
elms rising and slowly opening
familiar to you as breath.

If you lingered by them it was
only to raise a hand to your hair
and brush your absence away.
And then you turned
as you always turned, bent over
and touched my face.

Your step on the stairs
was definite, quick
going back to your own life.

6. We sit in a tide of sunlight
stealing across the surfaces
of the room, over board floors
and an ancestor's cupboard,
our mutually attentive faces
and fragile pulse of words.

Once more you speak
of small delights, the ones from which
you've crafted your life:
cosmos and peas and delphinium,
friendships flourishing in notes,
or the deer you saw flowing in a
neighbor's meadow.

Again I vanish behind a smile,
thinking I know your world
by heart.

It is the sun that pulls me back,
the simple pleasure of warmth
on my skin. For a moment
my blindness heals
and I look across to your eyes,
alive like quick soft animals
darting away from some sorrow.

What is it I long to ask,
wanting to hold you like my child
and brush aside the birthright of loss,

our need for reticence
or words.

WORLDS GREAT
AND SMALL

The Central Eye

Mother, should you come back again,
long after your pain has finished its feast,
after we've placed your porous bones
within the cache of earth,
I would wish for you some barbarous splendor,
some pride outrageous as the peacock's eyes
trailing copper and indigo
a powdery gold
through the lush heart of summer.

I would wish you to be
a caster of spells
or the child enraptured within them,
the child you were and always have been
reaching out through bars of light.
As when long ago in a neighbor's yard
you spied the royal birds.
And they stood for your touch,
they did not shy,
they moved like dancers of Krishna
gravely swiveling their heads.

Here, take this feather in your hand.
Hold it wherever you go—

The colors ring like oil on rivers
out from the central eye.
Do not be afraid of that blackness
where the first stirrings begin.
You have been there already, many times.
Its name is not always death.

Vermeer's Women

Caught in their daily grace
these female figures quietly astound.
They quicken with light
accepting its seeds
its oblique fall on skirts and rugs
on studded, blooming blues
on golds more subtle than desire.

They voyage inward
smoothly as bells
gliding from room to room,
superintending the rising
of bread of song
of their own clear flesh.

It is not
that they lack distraction.
Attentive to wine
or the quillscratch of love
they pause, perhaps for years,
then move on to their mirrors.

Unperturbed by centuries
they hold to their tiled ground
and stare through unsilvered glass:

decorous, swollen
unwitting vessels for the rest
who pour out their milk and music
their children, their blood
and are gone.

Looking at the Rembrandts

(Metropolitan Museum)

There is no way to evade
such faces,
such tender Inquisitors.

I look for answers
and find only naked eyes,
the grave composure

of a woman paring her nails
as another quite absently
holds out a pink:

the flower fringed and delicate,
impenetrable as fact.
I want only to turn away

from the pearls and filigree binding her hair,
the sorrow gleaming exquisitely
through her life,

but she claims me
and I linger,
dazed with recognition.

Somewhere in another room
a man looks up from study,
his aspect fine and rabbinical,

softened by too much knowledge.
His hands relax on a reading glass.
His ear is pierced discreetly with gold.

I turn with relief
to a coarse-featured man
who looks back with disgruntled wonder,

as if he were certain
of nothing at all,
as if his hands were blind to skill,

never knowing the maulstick or brush
or stroking our mortal light.

Slide Show

She flashed on to our kitchen wall,
a nude far gone in pregnancy
painted by Alice Neel. At first
she seemed all torso—huge colonized belly,
nipples standing erect as soldiers
above thin, shadowed ribs.
Her gaze, though, was strong as ours
undesperate and factual.
She knew she had no choices left.

No man I said
could have painted her.
No woman you answered
ever looked like that.

I called you stranger, amnesiac, a fool
who thought pregnant meant "in bloom."
But even as I ripened with anger
memories gathered for ambush.
I thought of your touch
in the labor room, how you
made up stories until I laughed,
how now you slowly trace those
marks, scars of our boundary crossing.

The Animals

(Circe speaking)
I did not ask them here.
They came in narrow ships—
Warriors
from the well-mapped world,
wanting only
to conquer and survive.

And I received them
generously, with rich meats
and honeyed wines,
listening for days on end
as they wove their butcheries
into legend.

Those
who did not interest me
I relieved of heroism,
making them snug
in their bristled pelts,
free to root and rut.

The others I knew.
Men bronzed and armored
in beauty
with the stamina of gods,

and with the seeds of fear
hidden deep in their eyes.

Now they are lions
and timber wolves, catamounts
down from the heights,
their claws sheathed
in my soft spells,
their teeth bared to mercy.

We meet deep in the forest
in clearings furred with light,
and throwing beast skins
and witch mask aside,
play at being human

becoming quick and soft
and imminent,
clear and terrified.
When I have had enough

I pick up my sorcerer's staff
and tenderly transform them
until once more they glisten as sons.
Their orange, elliptical eyes
brim with gratitude.

And I return
to this hearth, this loom,
the designs of solitude,
to pick the threads
of my own magic
and their interminable legends.

Otter Woman

it's such a relief to feel you are made of
much more than just yourself.
—Claire-Louise Bennett

I dreamed I was a river
and the river was my home
I left my wounds my clothes and my name
in a pile on its bank

I waded into currents
with arms crossed over my breasts
Soon they melded to a pelt,
dark brown and sinuous,
meant for slithering through rapids
and catching fish in my teeth

Otter Woman, that's who I was
sleek and long of spine
my country the Richelieu the Mississquoi
the Monongahela
All names I could not say,
my body too liquid for language

When I woke I missed those other names
so beautiful and syllabic
My clothes were too dry and too small

Even now I am drawn by moving waters
I give rivers and brooks great thanks

On Becoming an Apple Tree

Gradually
the graft takes hold.
I wake in disarray,
my limbs hard and opened, sprawling
into the orchard afternoons.
I feel my breasts and belly
amplify,
curve deeply into ripeness
becoming flushed, and heavy to bear.
As my roots grip the dark, dark earth
blood runs gold in my veins.

Touch is now only memory,
a necessity pruned away.
No hands trace round these scars
and gnarls. I am still
through autumn rains, blossomfall
the drowse of bees.
I am still
as the geese pass overhead,
dividing the highest winds
with their wild throats honking for joy.

Ode to Apples

Septembersap
Ninth-month fruit
Planets of skin and seed and juice
falling in orchards
from Shelburne to Eden
Gnarled marbles gone wild carpeting cellarholes
deep in the woods
where women lived
who rejoiced in your bloom
as the last of the snows,
an end to winters of roots and croup,
a resurrection of delicacy

Apples, apples
abundant as air
Most female of fruits
full of internal stars
Saucy, ruddy, firm of flesh
golden as myth or dream

Cider-makers
plump pie-bakers
succulent spheres
pleasing teeth and tongue
You are whole as love
tart as truth
crisp, available comfort

After Eurydice

I want to forget that mangled head
singing its song of no body, lost love

And hear the voices of those poor lost women
who tore Orpheus apart

What was it that they wanted, craved so dearly
they followed the other god?

I cannot believe it was just bloody obsession.
Rather, the lure of some undiscovered music

dimly heard in girlhood but not possessed,
of bees buzzing in the thyme underfoot

and the freedom to wander through it all,
purple fragrance, craggy goat paths, vistas of the
open sea.

Perhaps when they blossomed their lives
closed down,
mired in duties and expectations, or worse,
brutality

and the laughter which tenderness makes possible
never pealed from them, like the tolling of some
great bell

only higher and lighter.
The sound of reclaimed birthright

The Goddess Speaks

(from *Passage Tomb Series)*

I am She

who swells the moon,
casts its silver, reels the waves.
Through my labour all things form
and all life flows away.

I am fine as the tinge on the apple's flower,
serene as a fat white sow.
The flush on a young girl's cheek is mine
and the soft pull in her womb.

The bold who think they rule their lives
I tease with honeyed songs.
Their hearts become my dainty food,
their sea-washed ribs my harp

When the wind turns sharp I go to earth
beneath the unhewn dolmens.
I rise again with the barley in spring
and turn the grain to pearl.

I am close as the whorls
on your fingertips, far as the nebulae.
Trust this above all:
I am not what I seem

Through every change I abide.

The Deep One

is seized by a chill
as the voice of Marian Anderson comes over
                    the air
singing of sweet land of liberty
in 1939, at Lincoln's feet.

The notes throb and lift—
from fields where slave mothers stooped
their breasts swollen with newborns' milk

from cabins which whip-scarred rebels fled
in faith that Canaan existed on earth
somewhere beyond the Potomac.

As the song of freedom draws to its close
and rings from mountainsides,
the deep one dances on my skin,
every particle of her being alert to awe.

But sometimes, most times, the deep one hides
as she did last night in the bitter cold
as I hurried down a city street
on the way to meet my friends.

When a stubbled man stepped out of the shadows,
mumbling about coffee and need,
I pressed a quarter into his hand
and did not meet his eyes.
Safely past his filthy puff of jacket,
I began to hear the soft syllable *shame*
rising from within.

The deep one too has a beautiful voice
though I do not yet know her name.

Sifting

Snow falls through the shapely ash
outside my study window,
it falls on broader arms of pine
and through my seventy years

It falls and drifts inside me
past what it is that wants to clench
wants to guard against hope

past my hunch, reluctantly formed
that our human dazzlement with war
will outlast every season

past doubt that my work has
had effect, that my mind
is sufficiently lithe
to improve this or any white page

Unsent, unasked, the snow comes down
and falls to waiting ground

Meetings

Sometimes there were strangers in cities,
a man on a bus in Madrid—
those promenades of Goya and stone
where passion costumes as elegance.
I sat there rooted in motherhood
with my damply clamorous child,
and we looked across at each other
for block following block—directly
as man and woman, without homage
or shame or assault.

And you, with whom at first
I could not find words, with whom
I learned about retreat.
Streetlamps were softening into the mist,
the sidewalks iridescent, as we sat
in an empty West Side café
pretending to be somewhere else.
I kissed your palms and fingertips,
you stroked again the bones of my face—
as if to press such knowledge
into the scaffolding of our lives.

The Caged Woman

(inspired by Susan Glaispell's
"A Jury of Her Peers")

Now that the bars are actual, grippable,
made of iron and not of the scornful looks
and curt words of a man for whom
cruelty is less risky than tenderness,
she is free to search for her song.
No one will bother her.
Her arms, if she wants, will grow feathers
and her throat will vibrate to whatever is gestating
in her soul, if it has not succumbed to terminal
        stillness.
Her innocence lies lighter and deeper than guilt.

Will she find sorrow songs there, like the ones
Frederick Douglass overheard as a boy
when the slaves on his plantation were trudging
        through woods,
songs low and mournful, about generations
chained in Egypt Land?

I think not. I hear her voice high and clear
as her yellow bird's, a thing made of memory
blue ribbons and summer breezes,
a delicate thing like Mad Robin's, like the tunes
        of English country dance,
a thing that could cheer or waft away
compounded of heartbeat and breath.

Raincoat

It was a splurge, an Amsterdam splurge,
more than a hundred euros for its supple
        grey sheen,
a magnet for compliments and touch.
Practical too. Not only a hood but a visor.
Dry-eyed, dry-faced, I pedaled past tram stops
where the drenched and miserable huddled.

Every Mother's Day now
someone sends out Ada Limon's "The Raincoat"
and I am reminded
of what generous caregivers
my daughters are, especially the one
whose youngest had a double scoliosis
and a brace she wore to school every day
and toted to summer camp.

Raincoats, raincoats
warding off downpours.
Who protects the ones who hold them out?

Thought Experiment: Pitying Donald Rumsfeld (2003)

"We must learn to write love letters
to our President," said Thich Nhat Hanh,
who was no fool though he sounds one.
He witnessed, in June 1963,
his friend the abbot of Hué
hold a match to his saffron robe
in the center of Saigon
and make of himself a refiner's fire
to render cruelty from the hearts
of those who watched, whether near
or thirteen thousand miles away,
revealing in some
the slowly unfolding flower
which the Buddha calls compassion.

And so I guessed that accepting
Thich Nhat Hanh's suggestion
might exact something, that
finding commonality with one's enemies
required more than gracious intent,
but I asked myself why not, and why
not increase the challenge

by holding Donald Rumsfeld in mind
instead of George Bush
and his easy bafflement?
I was about to settle on a zendo cushion
for forty minutes of silence.

When I tried to summon
the child once Rumsfeld—
I expected a scraped-knees boy
whose tongue balked at prettified words—
he immediately ran away.
But seventy-four is just as vulnerable
as four, I told myself
so I called up an image from BBC:
a rumpled, stooped, probably
jet-lagged Donald Rumsfeld
walking towards some foreign podium
as if it were a station
on the way to the grave.

 Clichés about the human condition
swirled through my mind, and yes
I imagined us all standing in sorrow,
but the image did not touch my heart.

Many moments ebbed
before another image
bobbed up unbidden:

of two vertical panels hinged
like a Flemish diptych
with Donald Rumsfeld sitting at the upper left

in a slat-backed kitchen chair
as I, standing behind, placed
my fingertips on his temples
on the coves beyond the pulse's soft beat
and swept his hair back again and again,
to ease the pressure of having to be strong
of protecting the ungrateful.
To lighten the weight of hatred
it was his to bear.
When I stroked his closed eyes
my fingers discovered tears.

Just as the closing gong sounded
I dared a glance to the pit at lower right
where dozens of dark-haired
men women and children—
those we had planned to liberate—
were heaped on each others' stiff arms.
I recoiled, as if my shoulder
were hit by the butt of a gun,
and then I recoiled again,
appalled by my own smallness.

Though I am not sure
to whom I offer this prayer
I have faith that someone will hear

May our eyes stay open,
and may our hearts enlarge
to accommodate what our eyes take in.

Exodus

for Grace Lorch

I praise an ordinary woman,
greyblonde and stocky, nearing
forty, who stood as part of
a snarling crowd outside
Central High School in Little Rock
on September fifth, 1957.

She watched as eight
black teenagers (all chosen
for excellent grades)
got out of a Chevy wagon.
She saw them approach
the ring of Guardsmen
ordered to turn them away, saw
the crewcuts, the loose slung rifles
the fingers more used to basketballs
drumming on billy sticks.

When the eight faltered
and finally turned back
she may have helped scream them away.

And then she saw the latecomer ninth
walk into the spit of *Get Out!*
Go Back where trash belongs—
a girl named Elizabeth Eckford
in crinolines and a pressed white blouse
fifteen, too shy to bolt
the only black person in sight

And suddenly this unknown
woman, her face ambushed by pity
stepped out from the mob
and touched Elizabeth Eckford's shoulder

Made of herself a shield and wedge,
shamed her own to give way
and brought the girl out, through the bitter swell
roaring and closing
behind them.

Mose Wright Testifying
Bettman

The Witness

I give all praise to Moses Wright
who stood in 1955
where no black person had ever stood,
in the witness box of the courtroom
in Sumner, Mississippi.

Who stood calmly, without trembling
keeping a pastor's steady hand
on all the ghosts hungry for justice
eager to rise from within

Ghosts like Denby, a fieldhand
the boy Frederick Douglass saw shot
in the head by an overseer never brought to trial.

Like scores of Ibo who drowned by choice
in the surf off Sullivan's Island,
after weeks in a fetid hell.

Like the more than five hundred,
named and then recorded as nameless,
already lynched in Mississippi.

But Wright is here this day for one,
his fourteen-year old nephew Emmett Till,
down from Chicago for the summer
and abducted from his house at 2:00 a.m.
for the crime of touching a white woman,
placing coins for candy in her hand
and later, maybe, whistling.

It is nineteen days since the open casket,
more than three weeks since the killing,
long nights for Wright of hiding in his car,
sleeping with the dead by the rural church
where he used to preach.
Men with pistols had told him
you won't see the sun come up again
if you recognize us tomorrow

At last, on the trial's third day,
Wright is called to the stand—a slender figure
in a crisp white shirt, walking as if unafraid.
A man with a camera crouches in the aisle,
ready when the question is asked:
Do you see these men here?

Wright points and answers *Dar he*
Points and says *Dar he* again:
two short words
soon to be balanced against two others,
the verdict of the all-white all-male jury
whose brazen indifference trumps courage.

And yet not two months later,
when Rosa Parks, tired from her day's work,
decided to stay sitting, she thought of Emmett Till
and of the pain of justice denied.

And now, when I question almost everything,
I think of Moses Wright,
of his humble assurance,
of the well of gravity and dignity from which he drew,

and I give praise.

Dust

I woke up this morning with dust on my soul—
an ordinary occurrence, not a free fall
into the existential black hole which lies in
　　　　　the future
of collapsing galaxies, and maybe even of
　　　　　all creatures.
A future which manifests in the present
as utter loneliness.

No, this dust was ordinary, quotidian,
an accretion of motes, disenchantments
and the waning energies of age. Reflexively
I reached for the book on my night table,
Willa Cather's *Shadows on the Rock,* and
found there such a beautiful description
of winter light—the sheer feast of it—
that I was once more a child on a sled,
pushed off by my father.

Einstein too was a child on a sled
intimating the speed of light in his jostled bones
and the direction his life would take,
as his runners cleaved the ice-slicked snow
　　　　　beneath him.

In the northern winter sky
the Milky Way is a river of silver,
all the more wondrous because it is ragged,
partially obscured by clouds of dust
from ancient, pulverized stars. Beneath the clouds
                        are other stars
but theirs is a radiance inaccessible
to merely human eyes.

Arguing with Adrienne Rich

No! I shouted in pencil in the margin
when I read that birth stripped us of birthright

The orphan child of living parents,
my mother always knew what was hers: the gift
of life itself, with the right to open and use.
Without words she passed this on.

I watched her go about boring chores
and wondered why she was happy,
whistling as she unpinned sheets
from the wind's diligent breath,
as she smoothed out underwear and socks,
rolling compact balls of the mates.
The source of her stuttered songs
never seemed to run dry.

Repression too she passed on,
and an underground spring of sorrow—
but they weren't in my recent dream.

We were sitting on a Flexible Flyer a second after takeoff,
she the guide, blocking my view,
my child's arms gripping her as shield, as hedge
                against exultation
so as not to expire from joy and fear
as we bounced over ice pack and bumps

We were stars
                speeding down like starlight
                        not caring where to land.

For Willa Cather

1. Jaffrey Center, New Hampshire

Afraid, as you said
of dying in a cornfield,
you chose this harder place to rest,
among alien Starks and Shattucks
in the thin soil
and broken schist
beneath Monadnock's slope.

In this country, stones are earth
Rain glazes the old stained slabs
I pass on the way to yours.
It pools in the words chiseled
above you, proclaiming
"That is happiness, to be dissolved
into something complete and great."

Familiar words, easy to believe,
though I stand mute
and empty-handed,
wondering what people do at graves.

2. Interstate 80, Central Nebraska

Fiddling blindly with the knob,
I cannot find a station.
Only then do I look around, and recognize
I am nowhere
or somewhere on the floor of the sky.

Is this what you meant by
The Divide? This line where
prairie changes to plain
and wheat begins its yellow rise
towards the edge of the world?

Here one hundred years ago
you followed buffalo paths
through grama and bluestem and a coarse red grass
that at dusk darkened to wine.
Here Black Elk spoke his visions

and Démeter might have roamed
in search of a furrow
deeper than the rest,
where all that she loved went under.

Her keening was long ago lost on the wind
though here I listen for it.

Reading Du Fu

Heading east at thirty thousand feet
I lift my eyes from the page to hear
a temple bell—one clear lingering stroke
that rings over ridges of cloud.

Far to the south bloodorange light
narrows to a fiery band. I swirl
white wine in a plastic cup and muse
on family below. The child curled

in my daughter's womb, my husband's
aging father. Hunched over a still glad heart
he can barely climb the stairs. When will he
ever come to us or we go next to him?

We glide on beneath the Silver River
over constellations of towns,
jewels of cheer in a land pitch dark
and once more heading towards war.

Facing Snow

I raise a glass to this storm
which holds me in my housebound world
even as my mind goes out to the wind
and the waving woods by the brook

to the ridge beyond now blurred to sky,
pale grey and infinite. White freight settles
everywhere, and the driveway stays unplowed.
I'm free to go wherever I want.

Deeryard

On the way to the mailbox
I notice their sign—prints cloven
in fresh snow around an apple tree.
Only shriveled, high fruit remains.

Three winters ago
they graced us with their trust,
melting bowls in snowpack five yards
from the house, their hooves
tucked under like paws.

All of us under a cold moon
and light years from Orion.

Picnicking on Robert Frost's Lawn

for Judith

Mother's Day, the sky a blue bowl, the two of us
wanting to make a ceremony, or at least a memory,
though our children are miles and oceans away

and so we wind up Breadloaf mountain
to the Robert Frost Interpretive Trail,
a curated affair of poems on posts amid

rangy hemlocks, swelling nubs of wild
                    appleblossom
and the gurgling rush of a brook
nothing can stop or contain.

If the point of this expedition is to distract,
it works. I read aloud the words
of that craggy man who wrote in meter

quaintly rhymed "wither" with "thither"
yet said it All in five syllables.
Maple saplings, doomed by shade, hold out

their chartreuse palms, delicate as the
               white blossoms
of shad flourishing at the forest's fringe.
Shad . . . Vermont's sure sign of spring

and of spring melding with autumn,
               its bronze leaves
precisely the color of my daughter's once hair
and almost that of her dark honey eyes.

Later, wandering far off trail, we come to Frost's
summer cabin, where no one's in sight
on a long grassy slope spotted with dandelions

Profligate little suns! They're in our kingdom now
and it's time to open the rosé!
To Poets! we cry as we clink our glasses, *To Mothers!*

I want to add but my heart's not yet there
to the gold which cannot stay

A Catalogue of Cats

The first was a tiny white-pawed tiger
my father would not let me keep

Then poor Molly, pregnant too young
Her babies died undelivered
Mine, with forceps, arrived

That sleek fellow Othello
shat in a kind neighbor's slipper
when we were in Mexico

Oh Peter, smartest of all!
You learned to open cabinet doors
then sit in the dark and wait

Homer . . . my adored alpha male
needy, mouthy, carried and cuddled
Poison ivy bloomed on my chest

His brother was mild Beezus
a well-mannered hunter who ate his prey,
for a decade my significant other

And Oh Phoebe, cat of our hearts,
light was your only toy!
You chased the shadow of your tail

and the bright coin dancing on the wall,
cast from the crystal of my watch
as I sat grading papers

And now Mr. Muse, last of the line
Muzo the tawny one,
who gazes and gazes into my eyes

Flicks his thick tail
And bites

Elegy

For I will consider our cat Phoebe
who loved her life duly and daily
and honored the dignities of being a cat

She paused for ten seconds
at each morning's door,
that her chilled human might once again learn
the fiction of dominance

When she heard the sound of a patted lap
She paused for another ten,
and then, with gymnastical leap
accepted the proffered thighs

She knew the worth of her freedom
though her beauty she rolled in dust
which she licked from pussywillow feet,
permitting the praise of our touch

She would not have mousy baubles,
Light was her chosen toy--
a twinkle dancing on a wall
or the lure of her tail's own shadow

O lovely wreath of gray fur
Shy Goddess of the Hunt
Our guest, our familiar, our elegant other
we miss your grass-scented purr

Accommodation

The images we can't stop seeing
are not those caught by cameras.
My shots of a bleached Aegean, yours
of rust-streaked Turkish streets—
disappear at a finger's touch.

But how do we discard
the boy sobbing in Ankara,
sitting high on the overpass near Ataturk Bulvari,
his head a dark burr
pressed into the crook of our minds?
He guards his misery from the passing crowd
as if it were a golden egg.
No one tries to take it away.

We hurry by his heaving shoulders
and do not speak until we've
reached level ground.
Even then you speak first

as you do later, in Rhodes
after we've seen the Danish woman
for the third straight afternoon—
alone on the deck of her beat-up yacht,
her leathery, slightly fallen face
still fit for a prow.
She takes in cigarettes, retsina,

the routine assault of light.
How will she spend this wealth,
her life? She graciously smiles at us,
at the yapping pup at her heels.
You, son of a distracted mother,
can't put her out of your mind.

Home, we go about making this
home, having come together
in the middle of our lives.
Surrounded by so much to trust—
your words, my own, thirty acres of pasture
and a spring that's never run dry—
it still takes an act of faith

to bear our hollowed places
and accept each other whole.

Out the Window in Johnson, Vermont

January	triple birch shadow
	penciled on a blank white slope—
	Russia on our lawn

February	squeaky snow underfoot
	howls of a dog half-mile away
	black sky pricked with stars

March	mud, dreck, slop
	axles stuck in a deep rut
	I burst into tears

April	the falls' rush and tumble
	arrives through an open door—
	without the brook

May	a lattice of copper trees
	filters the rising sun—
	October in May

June   delicate laundry
              these prayer flags fluttering—
              who takes them in?

July   tree swallows swoop, dive,
              cruise through the evening
              squat in bluebird boxes

August   wind and leaves
              in a long conversation
              a cricket punctuates

September   early mists burnt away,
              the armada struts into view
              dark hulks bob and peck

October   open the glass doors!
              absorb the feast of color!
              stand there and give thanks

November   fields mowed to umber
              imminence in the chilled air
              we shore up our souls

December   a swift arc of rust,
              triumph in a cloud of snow
              my heart leaps with the fox!

Parkinson's Sequence

1. Complex and welcoming,
your beautiful hazel eyes
have not yet begun to take on
the sheen of glass

You look up from your plate
to meet me, and we share one more normal dinner,
questions and stories about our day
as a cello purrs in the background
and the pear candle on the table glows
    low and bright

Neither of us used to know
that normal is precious

2. The disease is the one with resilience.
we are the ones with our wind knocked out
only beginning to fathom
how to live with an inequality

3. Four years later, it is 6:15 a.m.,
in that lovely moment between
setting the mug on the table by my bedside
and taking the first sip of tea

that moment before my mind begins
to wander in replenishment
through the boundless grey fields of dawn
before gathering in for the day

in that sacred moment
you stir beside me, and
comings and goings become
an affair of wheelchairs

and gait belts and transfers
The bit tastes metallic
as I aim the big wheels
towards the bedroom door

Hours later, I remember something
You told me once, I think in bed,
the purpose of life is delight
and I think yes *yes*
and how delightful that you said it

GRIEF SEQUENCE

Homecoming

It's the proper season,
the ash trees, doomed and graceful
just beginning to turn yellow,
Canada geese heading south
over the lake, parents migrating to campuses
all over New England as I drive home
through the Intervale, returning
from speaking French with friends.

From somewhere in my aging brain
I'd resurrected words we once scrawled
on two sides of orange cardboard:
compass/la boussole, hike/la randonnée
trail/le sentier. But where is the trail
which leads through mourning?
Memories of Rousillon or Gordes intrude,
hill towns blessed with raw sunlight,
with the heat which still warms
the small, leaf strewn patio where
we delighted in quizzing each other.

Now, in the second before I remember,
I'm eager to tell you my triumphs.
I open the door to a mewing cat
and the sight of men's shoes by the hearth,

sandals meant for substantial feet
with toes inclined towards each other,
moved from the floor beside our bed
in the days right after you died.
I don't remember putting them there.

They make me think of Mary, the freer sister
who knelt to wash Jesus's feet
while Martha slaved in the kitchen.
And of all the mornings I knelt
to uncross the ankles your disease wanted crossed
before guiding your toes under straps.
It was a tender labor, half-desired.
Was I Mary or Martha or both?

In the kitchen I feed the cat
and pause to look out the window
before navigating riptides
of presence and absence in the other rooms.
Under us always, as if immortal
lies the brute fact.

Evocation

High summer's come round again,
July, the month of your death,
and those other, fabled Julys
when we used to jump backside first
into the flesh-shrinking cold
of the pool beneath the falls.

Where now to find the path?
I look for trampled grass
near the old orchard, around Nap Hill
down to a ferny bog
where you laid flat stones to lead us
into the shock of the green world—
cool, hemlock-filtered light,
the dappled rush of a brook
about to throw itself away.
Here sorrow is exiled.

Eons of needles cushion your step
as you go on ahead, mindful
now as ever to make the idyll safe.
You lift coiled rope from your shoulder
and loop it round a tree,
tugging it with broad-palmed hands
anchoring our slippery descent
through humus and roar and spray.

No nymphs or dryads await us
when we get to the pool's stone lip,
only a man who knows how to play,
who's in the water already.
A tiny submarine
sputters near his feet.

I want to rescue you from these waters
but you go off downstream, a tall figure
in barn boots who pauses to raise his head.

Is it the song, or a flash of yellow throat
high up in the canopy?

Post-Dawn

Most mornings I wake
empty of dreams, my imagination
a far off star on Orion's belt.
My first thought, often, is cancer,
my second how glad I am
not to believe in an omnipotent God
and have to explain suffering away

You could say suffering is the plot,
suffering leavened with joy
It's hard to be philosophical though
with a cat sprawled on my chest
his purr pressing my heart

Most mornings I throw
back curtains, and search for
the red bird perching on cottonwoods
swooping through cedars,
his mate a green gold beauty
who eschews proximity
and keeps faith from a separate tree

Some mornings my mind untethers
and moves beyond senses and sense
to the randomness of it all,
the dance of photons
hopping from orbit to orbit,

The All to the All

All shall be well
and all shall be well, and
all manner of thing shall be well
I whispered these words
to my brother as he was dying,
hoping Dame Julian could soothe
the question in his eyes
as our mother once stroked our tear-streaked faces
and penetrated our fears

Unknowing can be knowing
It's the dowry we bring
to drawing breath and suckling
to the subtle and unsubtle pleasures of love

I saw yesterday
a blind man standing before the
          Strasbourg Cathedral
singing simple prayers of praise,
his face turned towards the blue and the clouds
It's how he made his living
And I saw also Ste. Catherine
sitting in a nearby museum

with the same trusting, upturned face
sculpted from the local peach-colored stone
now thoroughly begrimed

I thought of my Katherine
now finishing her third round of chemo
whose future cannot be known

Christmas Night

The wind blows in darkness,
waving cottonwoods, roiling the lake
knocking trees over power lines just south of here
but we are an ark of warmth and light,
three generations born female,
chopping nuts and onions, celery and cheeses,
      whole handfuls
of herbs for our vegetarian feast
as we listen to Handel brighten the air, telling us
      over and over
that we have been given a child. A boy!

Presents, though, are the least of it.
As the last Hanukkah candles burn down
my knit-capped daughter withdraws
for her third rest of the day. She comes back
      for dinner
with long bronze hair, and later when we play
      Celebrities
she accumulates more than anyone else
of the white scrawled flakes we tossed in the bowl.
Knowing stars, bridging generations—Kate's the
      vital link.
When I draw Rihanna,"a figure in Welsh
      mythology"
no one knows who I mean.

After their mother bids them good night, my
      grandkids hang out and sing:
three siblings once three sisters, caroling
      glorias and city sidewalks
music riding their breath subsiding
Sad and serious and cherished
they lean towards each other on
      the old blue couch.
they are still within the ark
The wind blows and keeps on blowing

The Third Night

No need to hurry. No need to sparkle. No need to be anyone but oneself.

Virginia Woolf's words—written in a confident hand on a small chalk board above the radiator on the way into your kitchen, where you and your children would pass them several times a day. Your hand always steadier than mine, a hand for calligraphy and fine-tipped camel's hair brushes. When you were fourteen I paid you to design a placard for William Blake's words, *Energy is Eternal Delight.*

Now there are no words, no desires. They haven't been pummeled out of my skin; paralyzed rather by the police tape stretching across the future: *Do not enter. Nothing beyond makes sense.* I used to have a desire so strong and natural that I had no need to recognize it—a desire not to outlive my children. Now the endlessly accumulating present presses in and no one comes closer. You are gone.

I think of Woolf with her pockets full of stones, walking towards the cold beckoning river. It is March 1941, seven months into the Blitz, four months after my birth. Hard to believe, but that may have been a time worse than ours, Kate. Bombs again like swollen rain but not falling this time on us. Cold water, cold stones, pebbles on the beach by our house. Lake rocks, pretty zebra ones of quartz and slate, one now marking the grave of our last cat Miep. And ragged ones, the petrified mud that you preferred because you found fossils within. Drop them with force and there they were: shell prints small as a baby's thumbnail. Remnants of the Champlain Sea. No police tape barring the past.

You are ashes, your memory, your work an ember illuminating many. And now? The Hebrew words do not lie naturally on my tongue. I hold the shamash, bend toward the slim candles and all but one go out.

There are no words—you hadn't had them for days before your death. There is only light.

James Baldwin Looks at Me

From out of a burnished gold frame,
From an ink and wash portrait
which does not contain his gaze.
Anger softened by suffering emanates from it,
a directness searching and
uncompromised

Which I feel rather than see
because my eyes are lowered.
I'm sitting about two yards from his wall
aiming for that Buddhist one-pointed
       concentration,
the freedom of no-thought.
But Here, Now, distraction is more fruitful

I permit the steadiness of his gaze
to enter me.   I think of times in the past
when I must have turned to lovers
with some version of this gaze
and they asked "why are you looking at me
      that way?"
Why indeed? What in me sought the challenge?

And what in my daughter, whose
inelegant capable work-roughened hands
created this drawing, this print,
Who felt the necessity of pooling darkness

on the left side of Baldwin's face
and of bringing that darkness down to
the hollow of his throat, the organ of speech
just above his capacious heart?

"I can't be a pessimist because I'm alive,"
Baldwin said. She with her steady hands
gave form to his words. A quickening,
A flash of the mystery which beats
In us all and beat throughout her life.
And we felt seen.

Homage to Emily

Grief without loss—
vague and slippery and difficult to grasp,
unless it be the invisible caul or shroud
that enveloped Emily Dickinson
as she walked home from school in Amherst,
the only mourner among children
at home in this world

Or perhaps it is what I used to feel
sloshing within me, a great vagueness
I thought of as the Lake of Sorrow,
too vast to come from my life alone
A place where I knew I could drown
unless my toes could grip the muck
and propel me to light and air

That happened
and my cry when it came
was of joy mingled with sorrow,
called up rippling and flashing from an emptiness
like the immeasurable space between stars

Now grief washes into me in waves
all entangled with specific loss,
ordinary wriggling still quickening
with the lives it knew

And yet

I've heard this story twice,
once from a teacher decades younger than myself,
who spoke of a poor woman
holding her dead baby in her arms
bringing it to the Buddha
so that he could restore its life

He tells her I will, if you go round the village
and bring me back a mustard seed
from every family that has not
lost a loved one to death.

Her empty palms, when she returns
are no surprise to anyone
for she's absorbed the truth
we all know somewhere in ourselves,
that death is as common as birth . . .

Is this knowing balm for her heart?
It wasn't for mine.

. . . . .

My second teller
blew away the mustard seeds, and told me
what this woman was really sent to gather
were stories from every household,
some about infants with the soft fuzz
still on their heads matted by fever,

who didn't last the night,
Some about children effervescent with
        joy and song
suddenly made mute,
or about the old just trying to stare down pain

All were about how we walk and labor
in the valley of the shadow of death.
Sometimes our heads are anointed with oil,
my second teller said,
and sometimes they are not
but we are not alone
and if we listen we are balm

Daybreak II

The soul remembers everything
even what happens before language,
the things we can neither remember nor forget.
For me there were patterns of light playing on
       a crib quilt
shifting shadows of branches and leaves
a hush of voices outside the bedroom door
It was a gentle bliss

several decibels lower than the ecstasy on
       my face as a four-year old
the first time I saw the sea off New Jersey,
foam from the breakers lapping behind me.
I keep the photo on a nearby shelf
to remind me what is possible.

In another room, on a large canvas called Girl
       in Spring
twelve-year old Julian has almost the same
       expression—eyes all but closed
hair blown in the wind, a smile as if she knows
that old, archaic secret, that joy is at the
       heart of everything.

It emanates from the painting, disperses
       imperceptibly
into pure blueness of sky.

I think of the painter, her mother
of all our night feeds long ago, of how seriously
       this baby
took what she wanted, and afterwards when
       she smiled
how milk dribbled down her chin.

Her laugh, when it broke out weeks later
was a complete surprise. An infant can sound
       like this?
Reach so deep in her belly and peal, just peal?
It's taken me decades to recognize that place
as the emptiness where grief also lodges.

Coda: Musing on Bach

Music is its own mystery
It does not need words
to reconcile us to being here

It needs catgut, breath, finely shaved spruce
glue made from horses' hooves
skins stretched tight
fingers made agile by years of scales
to make
the wild looping energy of the Sixth Brandenburg
the excruciating tenderness of the Double Violin
     adagio
the place beyond sorrow at the end of the Mass in
     B Minor
which is achieved and perhaps forgotten,
leaving a residue

Is Bach indebted to God
or is God indebted to Bach?
wonders the endearing conductor
of the Netherlands Bach Society

Sometimes he sings along
as the music swells to finale

Acknowledgements

Some of the poems printed here have appeared in the following journals and anthology:

Green Mountains Review, Washington Review of the Arts, Sojourners, Calyx, West Branch, Feminist Studies, Medical Literary Messenger and *The Black River: Death Poems*. I thank their editors.

And I am grateful to the poets who've inspired me and whose words I've occasionally echoed. In two cases, the echo reverberates into the structure of my poem: Ursula Le Guin's "Song" in "Song for Julia"; and Christopher Smart's immortal and playful praise of his cat Jeoffry, who accompanied him to Bedlam and eventually wandered into my "Elegy."

* * *

Without listeners and readers, a poem is its own limbo. I give hearty thanks to the friends who've accompanied me through losses and learning and joys. Special thanks to Annemie Curlin, who read an earlier version of the manuscript; to Meg Pond, for her helpful intuitions; to Neil Shephard who suggested the title of the title poem; and most of all to Julia Alvarez and her generous spirit for a host of useful suggestions over the years. I'm also grateful to Lise Weil, Marcia Goldberg, Yehudit Silverman and other members of the Corona Writers' Group in Montreal for their warm support and spot-on sense of what works and what doesn't.

those infinitesimal, invisible specks of
light in every atom of everything:
us, trees, red bird, cats
even in the white palm-sized lake stones
marking our animals' graves